The Silver Fox's Guide to Modern Dating: Navigating Love and Relationships as an Older Man

By Sarah k.moore

Table of contents

Chapter 1. introduction to modern dating

Older men's modern dating.

The book covers a wide range of topics related to modern dating, including online dating, social media, texting, and more. It provides older men with essential advice on how to create a strong and attractive dating profile, how to communicate effectively with potential partners, and how to build meaningful connections with women.

In addition to offering practical tips and advice, the book also delves into the emotional and psychological challenges that many older men face when it comes to dating. It explores issues such as self-esteem, confidence, and fear of rejection, and provides strategies for overcoming these obstacles and building a successful dating life.

Overall, the purpose of Modern Dating is to provide older men with the tools and knowledge they need to navigate the modern dating landscape with confidence and success. By offering practical advice, emotional support, and psychological insights, the book aims to help older men build meaningful and fulfilling relationships with women in the 21st century

Changing nature of dating.

Dating has undergone significant changes in the modern era due to a variety of social, cultural, and technological factors. Here are some of the key reasons why dating has evolved in recent times:

Technology: The rise of digital technology, especially smartphones and social media, has transformed the way people connect with one another. Dating apps and online dating platforms have made it easier for individuals to find potential partners, and they have also expanded the pool of potential partners beyond one's immediate social circle.

Changing gender roles: The traditional gender roles of men as breadwinners and women as homemakers have shifted significantly in recent times. Women are now more likely to pursue careers and are financially independent, which has changed the dynamics of dating and relationships.

Changing attitudes towards sexuality: There has been a significant shift in societal attitudes towards sexuality, including increased acceptance of casual sex and non-heteronormative relationships. This has led to more open and diverse dating practices.

Delayed marriage: People are getting married later in life, which means they have more time to explore their dating options and experiment with different relationships.

Globalization: The rise of globalization and international travel has made it easier for people to meet and date individuals from different cultures and backgrounds.

Urbanization: The growth of urban centers has made it easier for people to connect with one another, and has led to a more diverse dating pool.

Overall, the combination of technological, cultural, and social changes has fundamentally transformed the way people approach dating and relationships in the modern era.

Older Men Struggle with Dating

There are several potential reasons why older men may struggle with modern dating:

Technology: Older men may not be as comfortable with using technology and dating apps as younger generations. They may also be less familiar with social media and online communication, which can make it more challenging to connect with potential partners.

Changing gender roles: Society's expectations of gender roles have evolved over time, and older men may not have adapted to these changes. They may still expect women to be more submissive or to take on traditional gender roles, which can create friction in modern dating relationships.

Different expectations: Older men may have different expectations for relationships than younger generations. They may be looking for a more traditional relationship or may not be interested in casual dating. This can make it harder for them to find compatible partners in a dating scene that has become more casual and focused on hookups.

Communication styles: Communication styles have also evolved over time, and older men may not be as comfortable with the more casual, informal communication that is common in modern dating. They may prefer more formal communication, which can create misunderstandings or make it harder to connect with potential partners.

Cultural differences: Depending on the individual's background and upbringing, older men may have different cultural values or beliefs that are not as compatible with modern dating norms. For example, they may come from a culture that places more emphasis on arranged marriages or does not prioritize dating at all.

It's important to note that these are generalizations, and not all older men will struggle with modern dating for these reasons. However, these factors can make it more challenging for some older men to navigate the dating scene and find compatible partners.

Chapter 2.Modern Dating Overview.

Modern dating can be complex and multifaceted, as it encompasses a wide range of approaches and experiences. Here are some key aspects to consider when trying to understand modern dating:

Online dating: The advent of dating apps and websites has revolutionized the way people meet and interact with potential partners. Online dating offers a vast pool of potential matches, but also comes with its own challenges, such as dealing with the pressure to present oneself in the most favorable light possible.

Casual dating: Many people are opting for non-committal relationships or casual dating rather than traditional monogamous partnerships. This approach can be liberating for some, but can also lead to confusion and emotional turmoil if expectations are not clearly communicated.

Communication: With the rise of digital communication, the way people communicate in dating has also changed. Texting and social media have made it easier to stay in touch with someone, but can also lead to miscommunication and misunderstandings.

Gender and sexuality: Modern dating has also seen a shift in traditional gender roles and the acceptance of a wider range of sexual orientations and identities. This has led to more open and inclusive dating experiences for many people.

Pressure and expectations: Modern dating can also come with high expectations and pressure to present oneself in a certain way or to adhere to societal norms. This can create stress and anxiety for some, especially if they feel they don't fit the mold of what is considered "normal" or desirable.

Ultimately, modern dating is a complex and evolving landscape that requires flexibility, open communication, and a willingness to adapt to new situations and experiences.

Tech's Role in Dating

Technology has revolutionized the way people date and find romantic partners. From online dating sites and apps to social media and messaging platforms, technology has made it easier for people to connect and communicate with each other.

Here are some ways technology has impacted modern dating:

Online dating sites and apps: These platforms have made it easier for people to connect with potential partners based on shared interests, preferences, and values. Users can create profiles, browse through matches, and communicate with each other through messaging and video calls.

Social media: Social media platforms such as Facebook, Instagram, and Twitter have become tools for people to showcase their personalities and interests, and connect with others who share similar interests.

Video calls: With the pandemic and social distancing protocols, video calls have become an increasingly popular way for people to communicate and connect with each other. This technology has allowed couples to maintain long-distance relationships and even go on virtual dates.

Texting: Text messaging has become a primary form of communication for many couples, as it provides a quick and convenient way to stay in touch throughout the day.

AI-powered matchmaking: Some dating apps are now using AI algorithms to match users based on their preferences and behavior patterns.

While technology has made it easier for people to connect and find potential partners, it also has its drawbacks. Some people may use technology to misrepresent themselves or engage in dishonest behavior, and it's important for users to be cautious and mindful of their online interactions. Additionally, the over-reliance on technology can sometimes lead to a lack of meaningful connection and emotional intimacy in relationships.

Social media and dating.

Social media has had a significant impact on dating in the modern era. Here are some ways social media has affected the dating landscape:

Increased Access to Potential Partners: Social media has made it easier to connect with people who share similar interests. With platforms like Facebook, Twitter, and Instagram, it's easier to find people who share similar interests, hobbies, and lifestyles.

Changing Communication Patterns: With the advent of social media, people have changed the way they communicate in relationships. Instead of talking on the phone or in person, many people now communicate through social media platforms, text messages, and other messaging apps.

Heightened Focus on Appearance: Social media has also created an environment where physical appearance plays a larger role in dating. Many people use dating apps and social media to present their best selves online, and there is a growing pressure to present a perfect image.

Greater Opportunities for Ghosting: With the ease of communication that social media provides, it's easier than ever to ghost someone. Ghosting is when someone suddenly stops responding to messages or calls, leaving the other person wondering what happened.

Increased Pressure for Public Displays of Affection: With social media, there is a pressure to publicly display affection and showcase your relationship online. Some couples may feel like they need to constantly post photos and updates to show that their relationship is going well.

Access to Information: Social media also provides access to more information about potential partners. You can learn more about someone's interests, hobbies, and values by looking at their social media profiles.

Overall, social media has had a significant impact on the dating world, changing the way people connect and communicate.

Impact of Dating Apps.

Online dating apps have had a significant impact on the way people meet and form romantic relationships. Here are some ways that these apps have influenced modern dating:

Increased access to potential partners: Dating apps have made it easier for people to connect with potential partners, regardless of their geographical location or social circles. This has expanded the dating pool for many individuals, allowing them to connect with people they may not have met otherwise.

Changing the traditional dating norms: Online dating has also challenged traditional dating norms and expectations, such as who initiates contact, how quickly to respond to messages, and how soon to meet in person. The ease of communication on dating apps has led to a shift in how people approach dating, with more emphasis on getting to know someone through messaging before meeting in person.

Facilitating casual hookups: Some dating apps are designed specifically for casual hookups and short-term relationships. This has created a new culture of dating that places less emphasis on commitment and more on casual encounters.

Increased use of technology in dating: Dating apps rely heavily on technology, such as algorithms and swiping interfaces, to match users and facilitate communication. This has led to a greater reliance on technology in dating, with some people preferring to use dating apps exclusively rather than meeting potential partners in person.

Potential for catfishing and deception: While dating apps have increased access to potential partners, they have also increased the potential for catfishing and deception. Some individuals may misrepresent themselves on dating apps, leading to disappointment or even danger for those who meet up with them in person.

Overall, online dating apps have had a profound impact on modern dating culture, shaping the way people meet and form romantic relationships.

Gender Dynamics in Dating.

 can be attributed to several factors. Here are some of the trends that have emerged in recent years:

Greater gender equality: With more women pursuing careers and financial independence, traditional gender roles in dating have started to change. Men are no longer expected to be the sole providers, and women are increasingly taking the lead in initiating dates and making decisions in relationships.

Increase in online dating: The advent of dating apps and websites has made it easier for people to connect with each other, regardless of their gender. Online dating has also helped to break down gender stereotypes and provided more options for non-traditional relationships, such as same-sex relationships and non-monogamous relationships.

Rise of feminist movements: The growing awareness of gender inequality has led to the rise of feminist movements, which have challenged traditional gender roles in dating. This has resulted in more women demanding respect and equality in their relationships, as well as more men becoming open to the idea of sharing household chores and responsibilities.

Shift in power dynamics: In the past, men were often seen as the ones with more power in relationships. However, this power dynamic is slowly shifting, with women gaining more control in their relationships. This is partly due to the rise of feminist movements and the increasing number of women who are financially independent and have their own careers.

Emphasis on consent: Consent has become a major focus in modern dating, with more people recognizing the importance of respecting their partner's boundaries and desires. This has led to a greater emphasis on communication, as well as the importance of having open and honest conversations about sexual preferences and expectations.

Overall, the changing gender dynamics of modern dating reflect a shift towards greater gender equality and a more inclusive understanding of relationships. While there are still challenges and inequalities that need to be addressed, these trends offer hope for a more equitable and respectful future.

Chapter 3. Preparing for Modern Dating

Prepping for modern dating.

Preparing for modern dating involves understanding the unique dynamics of dating in today's world and taking steps to navigate them successfully. Here are some tips to help you prepare:

Be aware of the online dating scene: Online dating has become an integral part of modern dating, and you should be familiar with popular dating apps and websites. Choose a platform that aligns with your dating goals and preferences and use it to connect with potential partners.

Practice self-care: Taking care of yourself is essential to be ready for the ups and downs of modern dating. This can include exercise, meditation, getting enough sleep, and practicing healthy habits.

Be clear about your expectations: Communication is crucial in modern dating, and you should be clear about what you're looking for in a relationship. This can help you avoid wasting time on partners who are not on the same page.

Keep an open mind: Be open to meeting different types of people and be willing to step outside your comfort zone. You may find that your perfect match doesn't fit the mold of what you thought you were looking for.

Stay safe: Modern dating can also come with risks, so it's important to stay safe. Be cautious when sharing personal information with strangers online, and always meet in a public place for the first few dates.

Don't settle: Finally, don't settle for less than you deserve. Be patient and keep looking until you find someone who aligns with your values and goals.

Remember that modern dating can be challenging, but by preparing yourself mentally and emotionally, you can increase your chances of success.

Growth Mindset in Dating

Embracing a growth mindset in dating means approaching dating as an opportunity for personal growth and learning, rather than focusing solely on finding a perfect partner or avoiding rejection. Here are some ways to cultivate a growth mindset in dating:

View failure as an opportunity for growth: Instead of seeing rejection or a failed date as a reflection of your worth, view it as a learning experience. Ask yourself what you can learn from the experience and how you can improve next time.

Focus on self-improvement: Instead of fixating on finding the perfect partner, focus on becoming the best version of yourself. This can involve working on your communication skills, developing your interests and hobbies, and investing in your personal growth.

Stay open-minded: Instead of having rigid expectations about what you want in a partner, stay open-minded and be willing to explore different types of people and relationships. This can help you discover new things about yourself and what you truly value in a partner.

Embrace challenges: Instead of avoiding challenging situations, embrace them as opportunities for growth. This could involve asking someone out on a date, trying a new activity together, or having difficult conversations with your partner.

Practice self-compassion: Remember that dating can be tough, and it's important to be kind and compassionate to yourself. Be patient with yourself and give yourself permission to make mistakes along the way.

By embracing a growth mindset in dating, you can turn the process of finding a partner into a rewarding journey of self-discovery and personal growth.

Overcoming Dating Anxiety.

Dating can be a source of fear and anxiety for many people. It's normal to feel nervous when you're meeting someone new and trying to make a connection. However, if these feelings start to interfere with your ability to enjoy dating and form meaningful relationships, it may be time to take steps to overcome them. Here are some tips to help you overcome fear and anxiety in dating:

Recognize your fears: The first step to overcoming your fears is to identify them. Think about what specifically makes you anxious when it comes to dating. Is it fear of rejection, fear of not being good enough, fear of vulnerability? Understanding your fears can help you address them more effectively.

Challenge your thoughts: Once you've identified your fears, take a step back and evaluate them. Are they based on facts or assumptions? Often, our fears are based on negative thoughts and beliefs that aren't rooted in reality. Try to challenge these thoughts by asking yourself if there's any evidence to support them.

Practice self-care: Taking care of your physical and emotional well-being is essential when it comes to managing anxiety. Make sure you're getting enough sleep, eating well, and exercising regularly. Additionally, engage in activities that make you feel good and help you relax, such as meditation, yoga, or spending time in nature.

Take things slow: It's okay to take things slow when you're dating. Don't feel pressured to rush into anything or to reveal too much about yourself too soon. Take the time to get to know the other person and build a connection at a pace that feels comfortable for you.

Seek support: If you're struggling with anxiety and fear in dating, don't hesitate to seek support. Consider talking to a therapist or counselor who can help you work through your fears and develop coping strategies.

Remember, it's natural to feel anxious when it comes to dating, but it doesn't have to control your life. By taking steps to address your fears and practice self-care, you can overcome your anxiety and enjoy the dating process.

Positive Dating Attitude.

Developing a positive and confident attitude towards dating can be challenging, but it's an essential step towards enjoying a fulfilling dating life. Here are some tips to help you build a positive and confident attitude towards dating:

Work on your self-esteem: If you struggle with self-esteem issues, it's important to work on building your confidence. Take time to appreciate your strengths, focus on your accomplishments, and acknowledge your self-worth.

Embrace the process: Dating can be a rollercoaster ride, with ups and downs. Instead of focusing solely on the end goal of finding a partner, try to enjoy the process of meeting new people, trying new things, and learning about yourself.

Be open-minded: It's easy to fall into the trap of having a specific idea of the "perfect" partner. However, being too rigid in your expectations can limit your dating pool and prevent you from meeting amazing people. Try to keep an open mind and give people a chance.

Practice communication skills: Effective communication is key to any successful relationship. Practice active listening, assertiveness, and empathy to build strong connections with your dates.

Set boundaries: It's important to establish and communicate your boundaries to potential partners. This will not only help you feel more comfortable and respected but also help you identify red flags early on.

Take care of yourself: Self-care is crucial for maintaining a positive and confident attitude. Make time for activities that make you feel good, such as exercise, hobbies, and spending time with friends and family.

Remember, dating can be a learning experience, so be patient with yourself, and enjoy the journey!

Dating: Preparing for Rejection.

Preparing for rejection in dating can be a difficult and emotional process, but it's important to remember that rejection is a natural part of dating and doesn't necessarily reflect your worth as a person. Here are some tips for preparing for rejection in dating:

Keep things in perspective: Remember that rejection is not a reflection of your worth as a person. It simply means that the other person may not be interested in pursuing a relationship with you. Don't take it personally and try not to dwell on it.

Manage your expectations: It's important to have realistic expectations when it comes to dating. Not every date or relationship will work out, and that's okay.

Try to approach dating with an open mind and don't put too much pressure on yourself or the other person.

Practice self-care: Taking care of yourself is important in all aspects of life, including dating. Make sure you're getting enough rest, eating well, exercising, and doing things that make you happy. When you feel good about yourself, rejection can be easier to handle.

Be open to feedback: If someone does reject you, try to take it as an opportunity to learn and grow. Ask for feedback on what you could have done differently or what the other person was looking for. This can help you improve your dating skills and be more successful in the future.

Remember that rejection is not the end: Just because one person is not interested in dating you doesn't mean that there's something wrong with you or that you'll never find love. Keep an open mind, stay positive, and keep putting yourself out there. You never know who you might meet next.

Chapter 4 . Creating an Attractive Dating Profile

Creating an Attractive Profile.

Creating an attractive dating profile is essential if you want to catch the attention of potential matches and increase your chances of finding a romantic partner. Here are some tips to help you create a compelling and appealing dating profile:

Choose the right profile picture: Your profile picture is the first thing people will see, so choose a clear, high-quality photo that shows your face and portrays you in a positive light. Avoid group photos or pictures where you are wearing sunglasses or a hat, as they can make it difficult for people to get a clear view of you.

Write a catchy bio: Your bio should be short, sweet, and memorable. Highlight your personality and interests, and try to show off your sense of humor or wit. Avoid generic statements like "I love to travel" or "I'm a fun-loving person" and instead provide specific examples that help people get to know you better.

Be honest: Don't try to present a false image of yourself in your profile. Honesty is important in any relationship, so be truthful about your interests, hobbies, and what you're looking for in a partner.

Showcase your unique qualities: What sets you apart from others? Highlight your strengths and unique qualities in your profile. Do you have a special talent or passion? Share it with your potential matches.

Be specific about what you're looking for: Don't be afraid to be specific about what you're looking for in a partner. Do you want someone who shares your love of hiking? Or someone who is family-oriented? Be clear about your preferences to attract the right people.

Proofread: Make sure to proofread your profile for any spelling or grammatical errors. A well-written profile shows that you're serious about finding a partner and that you care about the impression you're making.

Creating an attractive dating profile takes some effort, but it can pay off in the end by attracting the right kind of matches. Remember to be yourself, be honest, and showcase your unique qualities. Good luck!

Choosing the Right Platform.

Choosing the right online dating platform can make all the difference in your online dating experience. Here are some factors to consider when selecting the right platform:

Your Dating Goals: What are you looking for in a relationship? Are you looking for a long-term partner or a casual hookup? Different platforms cater to different audiences, so it's important to choose a platform that aligns with your dating goals.

User Base: Check out the user demographics of the platform. Is the user base mostly male or female? What is the age range? Are there a lot of active users in your area?

Features and Functionality: Different platforms offer different features and functionalities. Do you want a platform with a comprehensive matchmaking algorithm? Are you interested in video chat or other advanced communication features? Determine what features are important to you and look for a platform that offers them.

Reputation and Safety: Check the platform's reputation and safety measures. Look for platforms with robust security and privacy features, such as profile verification and SSL encryption.

Cost: Finally, consider the cost of using the platform. Some platforms offer free basic memberships, while others require a paid subscription. Determine what you can afford and what features you are willing to pay for.

By considering these factors, you can choose the right online dating platform that meets your needs and helps you achieve your dating goals.

Compelling dating profile tips.

Creating a compelling dating profile is essential for attracting potential matches and increasing your chances of finding a meaningful connection. Here are some tips on how to create a dating profile that stands out:

Choose the right photos: Your photos are the first thing people see when they come across your profile. Choose photos that are clear, high-quality, and show off your personality. Avoid group photos or pictures with filters that hide your true appearance.

Write a catchy bio: Your bio should be short and sweet, but also give potential matches a glimpse into your personality and interests. Be honest and authentic, and avoid generic phrases like "I like to have fun." Instead, share specific hobbies or activities you enjoy.

Be clear about what you're looking for: If you're looking for a serious relationship, say so in your profile. This will help attract people who are on the same page as you.

Use humor: A little bit of humor can go a long way in making your profile stand out. But be careful not to overdo it or come across as insensitive.

Avoid negativity: Don't use your profile as a platform to rant about past relationships or complain about your life. This can turn potential matches off and make you seem bitter.

Show, don't tell: Instead of simply saying you're adventurous or outgoing, give examples of things you've done that illustrate those qualities.

Be authentic: Above all, be true to yourself in your profile. Don't try to be someone you're not in order to impress others. The right match will appreciate you for who you are.

By following these tips, you can create a compelling dating profile that attracts the right kind of attention and helps you find the relationship you're looking for.

Dating Profile Photo Tips.

Choosing the best profile photo for dating is an important part of presenting yourself in the best light possible. Here are some tips on selecting the best profile photos:

Choose photos that are recent and accurately represent what you look like now. Avoid using photos that are outdated or heavily edited.

Use a mix of photos that showcase your personality and interests. For example, include photos of you doing your favorite hobbies or activities, traveling, or spending time with friends and family.

Avoid using group photos as your main profile photo. While it's great to show that you have a social life, it can be confusing for potential matches to figure out who you are in a group photo.

Make sure your photos are well-lit and in focus. Avoid using blurry or poorly lit photos.

Avoid using overly provocative photos or photos that could be considered offensive or inappropriate.

Include at least one close-up photo of your face, and one full-body photo. This will give potential matches a better sense of what you look like.

If possible, ask a friend to help you choose your photos. They may have a different perspective and be able to help you select the best ones.

Remember, your profile photos are the first impression potential matches will have of you, so it's important to choose them carefully.

Dating Bio Tips.

When it comes to crafting an engaging and attention-grabbing bio in dating, here are some tips to consider:

Be authentic and honest: Your bio should reflect your true personality and values. Don't pretend to be someone you're not or exaggerate your interests and hobbies. Authenticity is attractive and will help you attract the right matches.

Showcase your personality: Use humor, wit, or creativity to showcase your personality. For example, you can use a clever pun or a joke that reflects your sense of humor. Use language that makes you sound interesting and approachable.

Be specific: Instead of saying you enjoy "traveling" or "watching movies," be more specific about your favorite travel destinations or movie genres. This will give potential matches a better idea of your interests and can help spark conversations.

Avoid clichés: Try to avoid overused phrases like "looking for my partner in crime" or "I love to laugh." These phrases are generic and don't offer much insight into who you are.

Keep it concise: Your bio should be brief and to the point. Most dating apps have a character limit for bios, so make sure you use your words wisely. Focus on the most important things you want potential matches to know about you.

Use photos wisely: Your photos can also help showcase your personality and interests. Make sure they are recent and accurately reflect your appearance. Include photos that show you doing things you love, such as hiking or playing an instrument.

Remember, your bio is your chance to make a first impression on potential matches, so take the time to craft something that accurately reflects who you are and what you're looking for.

Chapter 5.Effective Dating Communication Strategies

Effective Dating Communication Strategies

Effective communication is essential for building and maintaining a healthy relationship. Here are some dating effective communication strategies that can help you develop a strong and successful relationship:

Active listening: It's essential to listen carefully to what your partner is saying, both verbally and non-verbally. Avoid interrupting or finishing their sentences, and don't assume that you know what they're going to say.

Use "I" statements: When expressing your feelings, use "I" statements instead of "you" statements. For example, say "I feel hurt when you don't call me back" instead of "You never call me back, and it makes me feel ignored."

Avoid blame and criticism: Instead of blaming or criticizing your partner, try to express your feelings without attacking them. For example, instead of saying "You're always late," say "I feel frustrated when we're late because it makes me feel disrespected."

Be clear and specific: When you're communicating with your partner, be clear and specific about what you want or need. Avoid vague statements or assumptions, and make sure your partner understands what you're asking for.

Practice empathy: Try to see things from your partner's perspective and understand their feelings and emotions. Be supportive and validate their feelings, even if you don't agree with them.

Choose the right time and place: When discussing important topics or sensitive issues, choose a time and place where you can both focus and have privacy. Avoid having these conversations in public places or when you're both tired or stressed.

Be open to feedback: Communication is a two-way street, and it's essential to be open to feedback from your partner. Listen to their perspective and take their feedback seriously, even if it's difficult to hear.

Overall, effective communication in dating requires patience, empathy, and a willingness to listen and understand your partner's feelings and needs. By practicing these strategies, you can build a strong and healthy relationship based on open and honest communication.

Dating: Importance of Communication

Understanding the importance of communication in dating

Effective communication is crucial in any relationship, especially in dating. It helps partners understand each other's thoughts, feelings, and needs. Good communication in dating can help build trust, deepen emotional connections, and avoid misunderstandings.

Here are some reasons why communication is essential in dating:

Builds trust: Open and honest communication is key to building trust in a relationship. When partners communicate effectively, they learn to rely on each other and build a strong foundation for a healthy relationship.

Enhances emotional intimacy: Communication helps partners get to know each other better, which can lead to deeper emotional connections. When partners feel comfortable sharing their thoughts and feelings, they become more emotionally intimate, which can strengthen the relationship.

Avoids misunderstandings: Misunderstandings can often arise in relationships when partners fail to communicate effectively. By communicating clearly and honestly, partners can avoid misunderstandings and work together to resolve any issues that may arise.

Resolves conflicts: Conflicts are a natural part of any relationship. Effective communication can help partners navigate conflicts in a healthy way, by expressing their feelings and needs without attacking or blaming each other.

Encourages growth: Good communication can also help partners grow individually and as a couple. By sharing their goals, dreams, and aspirations, partners can support each other in achieving their full potential.

In conclusion, effective communication is critical in dating, as it can help build trust, enhance emotional intimacy, avoid misunderstandings, resolve conflicts, and encourage growth. Partners who communicate openly and honestly are more likely to build strong, healthy relationships that last.

Dating Conversation Tips.

Mastering the art of conversation is crucial for dating success. It's not just about saying the right things, but also about listening actively, showing genuine interest, and connecting on a deeper level. Here are some tips for improving your conversational skills in dating:

Ask open-ended questions: Ask questions that encourage your date to elaborate and share more about themselves. Avoid yes/no questions and instead ask questions that require more thoughtful answers. For example, instead of asking "Do you like movies?" try "What's your favorite movie and why?"

Listen actively: Pay attention to what your date is saying and respond appropriately. This means making eye contact, nodding, and responding with follow-up questions or comments. Don't interrupt or talk over your date.

Share your own stories: Conversation is a two-way street, so be sure to share your own stories and experiences as well. This can help build rapport and create a more relaxed and comfortable atmosphere.

Avoid controversial topics: While it's important to have meaningful conversations, it's best to avoid controversial or sensitive topics like politics, religion, or exes. These topics can lead to disagreements and awkward moments.

Show interest and enthusiasm: Show your date that you're interested in what they have to say by asking questions, making eye contact, and responding with enthusiasm. Smile, laugh, and be engaging.

Be yourself: Don't try to be someone you're not in order to impress your date. Be authentic and genuine, and let your personality shine through.

Remember, the art of conversation is all about building connections and getting to know someone on a deeper level. By asking thoughtful questions, listening actively, and sharing your own experiences, you can create a memorable and enjoyable dating experience.

Dating: Navigating Difficult Conversations.

Navigating difficult conversations in dating can be challenging, but it's an essential part of building a healthy and fulfilling relationship. Here are some tips to help you navigate these conversations:

Choose the right time and place: Make sure you choose a time and place where you both feel comfortable and can speak freely without interruption or distraction. Avoid having these conversations when you or your partner are tired, stressed, or distracted.

Be honest and direct: It's important to be honest and direct about your thoughts and feelings. Avoid being passive-aggressive or beating around the bush, as this can lead to misunderstandings and hurt feelings.

Listen actively: Listen to what your partner has to say and try to understand their perspective. Don't interrupt or dismiss their feelings, even if you don't agree with them.

Avoid blame and criticism: Instead of blaming or criticizing your partner, focus on expressing your own feelings and needs. Use "I" statements instead of "you" statements to avoid making your partner feel defensive.

Take a break if needed: If the conversation becomes too heated or overwhelming, it's okay to take a break and come back to it later when you both feel calmer and more centered.

Seek outside help if necessary: If you're having difficulty navigating a difficult conversation, consider seeking the help of a therapist or counselor. They can provide an objective perspective and help you work through any issues that may arise.

Remember, difficult conversations are a normal and necessary part of any relationship. By approaching these conversations with honesty, respect, and empathy, you can build a stronger and more fulfilling connection with your partner.

Dating nonverbal cues.

Nonverbal communication is an essential aspect of dating because it provides additional information that complements what is being said verbally. Recognizing nonverbal cues can help you understand your date's feelings, intentions, and level of interest. Here are some nonverbal communication cues to look out for in dating:

Eye contact: Eye contact is a powerful nonverbal communication cue. If your date maintains good eye contact, it shows that they are engaged in the conversation and interested in what you are saying.

Facial expressions: Facial expressions can tell you a lot about your date's emotions. For example, if they smile often, it could mean they are happy and enjoying the date. On the other hand, if they furrow their brows, it could indicate they are confused or not interested.

Body language: Pay attention to your date's body language, including their posture, gestures, and movements. For instance, if they lean in towards you, it could indicate they are interested in you. Conversely, if they lean away or cross their arms, it could mean they are uncomfortable or disinterested.

Tone of voice: The tone of your date's voice can reveal their emotions and intentions. A warm and enthusiastic tone can indicate they are interested in you, while a monotone or flat tone could mean they are bored or disengaged.

Touch: Touch can also convey a lot of nonverbal communication cues. If your date touches your arm or hand during the conversation, it could mean they are trying to connect with you.

Remember, nonverbal cues should be considered in context and should not be taken as definitive signs.

Always pay attention to verbal communication as well, and use your own judgment to interpret your date's behavior.

GLUTEN FREE GUT HEALTH COOKBOOK

Healthy Gluten-Free Recipes for Gut Vitality

CHRISTIANA WHITE

GAIN ACCESS TO MORE BOOKS

TABLE OF CONTENTS.

4

Chapter 6.Healthy Dating Relationships

Healthy Dating Relationships.

Building and maintaining healthy relationships in dating requires effort and commitment from both partners. Here are some tips to help you build and maintain healthy relationships in dating:

Communication: Communication is key to building and maintaining healthy relationships. Be honest and open with your partner about your feelings, thoughts, and expectations. Listen actively to your partner and try to understand their perspective.

Respect: Respect your partner's boundaries, opinions, and decisions. Treat them with kindness, empathy, and compassion.

Trust: Trust is an essential ingredient in any healthy relationship. Be reliable, honest, and dependable. Avoid lying, cheating, or betraying your partner's trust.

Compromise: Compromise is essential to resolving conflicts in healthy relationships. Try to find a middle ground that satisfies both partners' needs and desires.

Spend quality time together: Spend time doing things you both enjoy and make an effort to create new shared experiences. This can help deepen your connection and create lasting memories.

Be supportive: Support your partner in their personal and professional goals. Encourage them to pursue their passions and dreams.

Practice forgiveness: Forgiveness is essential in any relationship. When conflicts arise, try to forgive and move forward. Avoid holding grudges or bringing up past mistakes.

Seek professional help: If you're struggling to build or maintain a healthy relationship, consider seeking professional help. A therapist or counselor can help you identify the root causes of your issues and provide strategies to overcome them.

Remember that building and maintaining healthy relationships takes time and effort. Be patient, understanding, and committed to making your relationship work.

Dating Relationship Stages.

Dating and relationships can be complex, but generally speaking, there are several stages that many relationships go through as they develop. It's important to note that not all relationships follow the same pattern or timeline, and individuals may experience these stages in different ways or skip some altogether.

Here are some common stages of a relationship in dating:

Attraction and Infatuation: In this initial stage, you may feel a strong attraction to someone and experience intense feelings of infatuation or "butterflies in your stomach." This is often fueled by physical attraction and the excitement of getting to know someone new.

Getting to Know Each Other: As you spend more time together, you start to learn more about each other's personalities, interests, and values. This is a time for building a deeper connection and deciding whether you're compatible.

Building a Relationship: If you both decide to pursue a relationship, you'll start to build a stronger connection by spending more time together, sharing experiences, and creating memories. This is a time to develop trust, communication skills, and emotional intimacy.

Commitment: After several months or years of dating, you may decide to take your relationship to the next level by becoming exclusive, moving in together, getting engaged, or getting married. This stage represents a deeper commitment and a long-term vision for your future together.

Maintaining a Relationship: Once you're in a committed relationship, you'll need to work on maintaining your connection over time. This means continuing to communicate openly, supporting each other through ups and downs, and investing in your relationship by doing things together and prioritizing quality time.

It's worth noting that not all relationships will progress through each of these stages, and some relationships may end before reaching certain milestones. It's important to communicate openly with your partner and be willing to adjust your expectations and goals as your relationship evolves.

Dating intimacy tips.

Developing intimacy and connection in dating is essential for building a strong and healthy relationship. Here are some tips on how to do that:

Communicate: Communication is key to building intimacy and connection. Be open and honest about your thoughts, feelings, and desires. Listen actively to your partner, and try to understand their perspective.

Spend quality time together: Make time for each other and engage in activities that you both enjoy. This can be anything from going for a walk in the park, trying out a new restaurant, or just staying in and watching a movie.

Show affection: Small gestures of affection, such as holding hands or giving a hug, can go a long way in building intimacy and connection.

Share your vulnerabilities: Sharing your vulnerabilities with your partner can help deepen your connection. Be willing to be vulnerable and share your fears, insecurities, and past experiences.

Be supportive: Show support for your partner by being there for them when they need you. This can be as simple as offering a listening ear or providing encouragement when they are facing a challenge.

Practice empathy: Try to see things from your partner's perspective and practice empathy. This can help you understand them better and build a stronger connection.

Remember that building intimacy and connection takes time and effort. Be patient, be willing to work on your relationship, and enjoy the journey together.

Dating Conflict Navigation

Navigating conflicts in dating can be a challenging experience, but there are several strategies you can use to help resolve conflicts and maintain a healthy relationship. Here are some tips:

Communicate openly and honestly: Clear communication is essential in any relationship. Be open and honest with your partner about your feelings and concerns, and encourage them to do the same. Try to listen actively and avoid interrupting or getting defensive.

Take responsibility for your actions: If you have made a mistake, take responsibility for it and apologize sincerely. Avoid blaming your partner or making excuses.

Find common ground: Look for areas where you and your partner can agree, and focus on those areas. It is okay to disagree on certain things, but try to find a compromise or a way to work together.

Take a break: If you find yourselves getting too heated or emotional, take a break from the conversation. This can help you both cool down and approach the issue with a clear head.

Seek outside help: If you are having trouble resolving a conflict, consider seeking outside help. This could include a therapist, mediator, or trusted friend or family member.

Remember, conflicts are a normal part of any relationship, and it's how you handle them that matters. With open communication, empathy, and a willingness to work together, you can navigate conflicts in dating successfully.

Dating: Independence and Interdependence.

Balancing independence and interdependence in dating can be challenging, but it is essential for a healthy and fulfilling relationship. Independence means having your own interests, goals, and values, and being able to make your own decisions without relying solely on your partner. Interdependence, on the other hand, means being able to rely on your partner and work together as a team.

Here are some tips for balancing independence and interdependence in dating:

Communicate openly: Communicate openly with your partner about your needs and expectations. Let them know what you need from the relationship to feel independent and what you need to feel connected.

Take time for yourself: Make sure to take time for yourself to pursue your interests and hobbies. This will help you maintain your independence and keep your own identity.

Spend quality time together: Make time to spend quality time with your partner. This will help you feel connected and build a stronger relationship.

Trust and respect: Trust and respect are essential for any healthy relationship. Trust your partner to make their own decisions and respect their independence.

Support each other: Be supportive of each other's goals and interests. Encourage each other to pursue your dreams and help each other achieve them.

Set boundaries: Setting boundaries is crucial in any relationship. Establish boundaries that allow you to maintain your independence while also being connected to your partner.

Remember, finding the right balance between independence and interdependence takes time, effort, and communication. Be patient with each other, and work together to build a strong and healthy relationship.

Chapter 7.Navigating Challenges in Modern Dating

Navigating Challenges in Modern dating.

Modern dating can be both exciting and challenging. While technology has made it easier to meet new people, it has also created new problems and obstacles that can make dating a daunting task. Here are some tips for navigating challenges in modern dating:

Establish clear communication: In modern dating, there are a lot of unspoken rules and expectations. It's important to establish clear communication with your partner about what you are looking for and what you expect from the relationship. This can help avoid misunderstandings and prevent hurt feelings.

Be authentic: With the rise of social media, it can be easy to present a curated version of yourself. However, it's important to be authentic when dating. Being yourself can help you attract the right people and build meaningful connections.

Be mindful of safety: Online dating can be a great way to meet new people, but it's important to be mindful of safety. Always meet in public places, let someone know where you are going, and trust your gut if something doesn't feel right.

Take it slow: Modern dating can often feel fast-paced, but it's important to take your time and not rush into things. Getting to know someone takes time, and it's important to build a strong foundation before diving into a relationship.

Keep an open mind: Modern dating can be full of surprises, so it's important to keep an open mind. Be willing to try new things and meet new people, even if they don't fit your preconceived notions of what you are looking for.

Practice self-care: Dating can be emotionally taxing, so it's important to take care of yourself. Make sure you are taking time to do things you enjoy and to practice self-care. This can help you feel more balanced and grounded during the ups and downs of dating.

Overall, navigating challenges in modern dating requires patience, communication, and a willingness to be open-minded. By taking these steps, you can increase your chances of building meaningful connections and finding love.

As people age, it's common to experience insecurities related to dating. These insecurities can stem from a variety of factors, such as physical appearance, career success, financial stability, and overall life experiences. Here are some tips for addressing age-related insecurities in modern dating.

Focus on self-improvement: Instead of fixating on your insecurities, focus on improving yourself. Take up a new hobby, learn a new skill, or work on your physical health. Doing so will not only help you feel more confident, but it will also make you more interesting to potential partners.

Embrace your age: Aging is a natural part of life, and there's nothing wrong with getting older. In fact, many people find that they become more confident and comfortable in their own skin as they age. Embrace your age and the life experiences that come with it, and don't be afraid to show your true self to potential partners.

Be open-minded: Don't limit yourself to dating only people your own age. Be open-minded and consider dating people who are younger or older than you. You may be surprised at how much you have in common with someone who is outside of your age range.

Don't compare yourself to others: It's easy to feel insecure when you see other people who seem to have it all together. However, it's important to remember that everyone has their own journey in life. Don't compare yourself to others, and focus on being the best version of yourself.

Communicate your feelings: If you're feeling insecure about your age or any other aspect of your life, it's important to communicate those feelings to your partner. They may be able to provide you with reassurance and support, and it can also help to strengthen your relationship.

Remember, everyone has their own insecurities, and it's important to address them in a healthy way. By focusing on self-improvement, embracing your age, being open-minded, avoiding comparison, and communicating your feelings, you can overcome age-related insecurities and enjoy a fulfilling dating life.

Overcoming the fear of commitment in dating

The fear of commitment in dating is a common issue that many people face. It can arise from a variety of reasons, such as past relationship traumas, fear of losing independence, or simply the uncertainty of whether a long-term commitment is the right choice.

If you're struggling with the fear of commitment, here are some strategies that may help you overcome it:

Identify the source of your fear: Understanding the underlying reasons behind your fear of commitment can help you work towards resolving them. Take time to reflect on your past experiences and any potential factors that may be contributing to your fear.

Communicate with your partner: Be open and honest with your partner about your concerns. Discuss your feelings and thoughts about commitment and try to come to a mutual understanding. This can help alleviate some of the pressure and uncertainty you may be feeling.

Take things slow: It's okay to take your time and not rush into a commitment. Focus on building a strong foundation for your relationship, and take things one step at a time. This can help you feel more comfortable and confident in the relationship.

Practice self-care: Make sure to prioritize your own needs and well-being. This can include activities such as exercise, meditation, or spending time with friends and family. Taking care of yourself can help you feel more grounded and less anxious about the future.

Seek professional help: If your fear of commitment is causing significant distress or interfering with your ability to form meaningful relationships, consider seeking the help of a therapist. A mental health professional can work with you to identify and address any underlying issues and provide you with tools and strategies to overcome your fear.

Remember, overcoming the fear of commitment is a process that takes time and effort. Be patient with yourself, and don't be afraid to seek support along the way.

Managing expectations and dealing with disappointment in dating

Managing expectations and dealing with disappointment in dating can be challenging, but it's an important part of the process. Here are some tips to help you navigate these situations:

Be clear about your expectations: Before entering into any dating situation, it's important to be clear about what you want and what you're looking for. This can help you avoid getting into relationships that aren't a good fit and can also help you manage your expectations.

Be realistic: It's important to be realistic about what you can expect from a potential partner. No one is perfect, and everyone has flaws. It's important to accept that you may not find someone who meets all of your criteria, and that's okay.

Communicate openly: Communication is key in any relationship, and it's especially important when managing expectations and dealing with disappointment. If you're feeling let down or disappointed by something your partner has done, it's important to communicate your feelings in a clear and non-accusatory way.

Take responsibility for your own feelings: It's important to remember that you are responsible for your own feelings. If you're feeling disappointed or let down, it's important to acknowledge and work through those feelings on your own, rather than expecting your partner to fix them for you.

Take time for self-care: Dealing with disappointment can be tough, but it's important to take time for self-care. This might mean taking a break from dating for a while, spending time with friends and family, or engaging in activities that bring you joy.

Remember, dating can be a rollercoaster of emotions, but with the right mindset and tools, you can navigate it successfully.